Love Calls

Narrow the road that leads to life

Matthew 7.14

SUSAN J. RICHARDSON

C P
THE CHOIR PRESS

First published in the United Kingdom in 2020 by
The Choir Press

ISBN 978-1-78963-110-4

A selection of these poems have been previously published in Rainbows in the Night: Matador Publishing

Contents

At last I have found my calling!
My calling is love!
Therese de Lisieux

LOVE CALLS

In a cloud of glory
Love's face is now
hidden from sight.

A silent veil of mystery
shades the brilliance of
the morning light.

Raindrops, red with
noon-day passion,
fall upon earth's ghostly
grave.

Songs of adoration
rise from the heart of
a maiden,
overshadowed by Love.

Seas and rivers,
mountains and valleys,
men and beasts,
all created at Love's
behest.

Rivers rise, crops fail
and disease leaves a
trail of death in its wake.

War and rumours of war
entrap mankind
in a deadly
web of anxiety.

Fortunes come and go,
maestros of the city
conduct their business
with uncontrolled alarm.

Shepherds of church
and state,
ever dreaming of a new
Utopia,
spin faster and faster with
every passing fear.

Far, far beyond the storms
and troubles of this world,
enthroned in eternal splendour,
the still small voice of Love
calls to one and all:

**'Come to me, all you who are
weary and burdened,
and I will give you rest.'**
Matthew 11.28

Love is the first and foremost call of every Christian, a call to share in God's unfailing love for this fallen world, but what exactly do we mean by love?

God's love is far from the world's counterfeit ideas of love. God's love seems scandalous with its call to love our enemies and do good to those who hate us. It is a love that is not of this world, a love which is far wider, longer, deeper and higher than we can imagine, a love which surpasses all knowledge. (Ephesians 3)

There is an enemy, who has many names, the Father of Lies, the Prince of this World, Satan, the Evil one, who will use everything and anything to stop us walking along the narrow way of love. If, however, we are serious in our desire to follow Christ then travel this way we must. Love, mercy and forgiveness are not optional extras in the Christian life, they are the very essence of it.

Anger, violence, hatred and a desire for revenge on enemies destroy thousands and thousands of lives every day. Some are physically destroyed or scarred, others mentally, emotionally and spiritually. Anger, hatred and revenge do not bring healing to our troubled world or individuals, they just beget more hatred and violence.

The Christian call of love is not a fair weather call. It is the way we are called to live in every moment of every day whatever the circumstances.

Love is as much about who we are as what we do. God Is love and we are made in his image. One does not have to look far to realise that image has been marred. In turn this leads us to a distorted view of love.

We seem to be forever starting from the wrong place in this matter of love. Love begins with knowing God's love for the fallen world and all his people. '**We love because he first loved us.**' *1 John 4.19*

When I was younger I found the words in John's Gospel about the disciple whom Jesus loved puzzling (John 13.23) Did Christ not love all his disciples? As I prayed about this it came to me that this disciple was the one who allowed himself to be loved.

We are not loved because of anything we have done or not done but because we are the offspring of God's love.

It is not possible to know ourselves loved, sins and all, and not desire others to know this love. In the Gospel Christ, speaking to the Pharisees said **"I tell you the truth, the tax collectors and prostitutes are entering the kingdom of God ahead of you."**
Matt.21.31

The prostitutes and tax collectors knew their need of God's unconditional love and mercy. The Pharisees thought they had a right to enter the kingdom because they were not really sinners. They fasted twice a week, tithed their income and kept the commandments, but they did not know their need of God's forgiveness and mercy. At the banquet when a sinful woman anointed the feet of Christ there was much tut-tutting. Christ said:

> **Therefore, I tell you her many sins have been forgiven – for she loved much. But he who has been forgiven little loves little.**
> *Luke 7.47*

Lord, in your mercy grant us to know our own need for forgiveness and mercy that we might love much. Amen

LOVE

And now I will show you the most excellent way. If I speak in the tongues of men and angels, but have not love, I am only a resounding gong or a clanging cymbal. If I have the gift of prophecy and can fathom all mysteries and all knowledge, and if I have a faith that can move mountains, but have not love, I am nothing. If I give all I possess to the poor and surrender my body to the flames, but have not love, I gain nothing.

Love is patient, love is kind, it does not envy, it does not boast, it is not proud. It is not rude, it is not self-seeking. It is not easily angered, it keeps no record of wrongs. Love does not delight in evil but rejoices with the truth. It always protects, always trusts, always hopes, always perseveres.

Love never fails. But where there are prophecies, they will cease; where there are tongues, they will be stilled; where there is knowledge, it will pass away. For we know in part and we prophesy in part, but when perfection comes, the imperfect disappears. When I was a child, I talked like a child, I reasoned like a child. When I became a man, I put childish ways behind me. Now we see but a poor reflection in a mirror; then we shall see face to face. Now I know in part; then I shall know fully, even as I am fully known.

And now these three remain: faith, hope and love.
But the greatest of these is love.
        1 Corinthians 13

THE RULE OF LOVE

The Rule of Love begins
with a heart centred on God,
for all love must be chaste,
not deceived by the world's embrace.

Love which is not in accordance
with the Father's will
in time and place
is not love at all,
but rather
the seeking of righteousness
in the market place.

Love, centred on God,
fears not the loss of face,
has no desire to be centre stage;
instead,
relies on him alone to
present its case.
The demands of love
are truth and grace,
the doorway to the garden of poverty.

It is in this garden of poverty
where the choicest fruits
of patience, goodness and humility
will grow.

Possessing nothing of our own:
then in abundance
the seeds of his fruit
will the Spirit sow.
A garden still well stocked with
the fruits of human effort
leaves no space
for the sowing of the Spirit.

In the garden of poverty
grow the flowers of freedom –
no weeds of fear and doubt
nor the slugs of 'should' or 'ought.'
No conditions,
be it cold and stormy
or hot and dry
will stop the blossoming of these
flowers.

Love, now chastened
by the belt of poverty,
is unlocked with the key
of obedience.
No longer now
do we need protecting
from the lust of the world's embrace.
Naked now in God's glory,
we can withstand the trials and temptations
of status, pride and vain glory.

The vows of chastity,
poverty and obedience
are not rules to be imposed,
but rather
Heaven's Courts
in which to live, to work
and play.

It was the heart of man
that nailed the Saviour
to the Cross.
It is the heart of man
that lifts him higher.

Not my will,
but thine O Father.
Not my will
but thine O Lord

PART ONE

The Narrow Way

Autobiographical Landmarks

Enter through the narrow gate.
For wide is the gate and broad is the road
that leads to destruction,
and many enter through it.
But small is the gate and narrow the road
that leads to life,
and only a few find it.

Matthew 7.13-14

INTRODUCTION

In 1989 several friends urged me to write down some of what I had seen in and through the ups and downs of my life.

I offered up a prayer about whether this was the right thing to do and how to do it. A week or two later 'bundles of words' complete with titles, began to surface in my mind. This was not quite what I had expected but then I have found that often to be the case.

Over the years people have asked me to explain some of these bundles. Pondering on this I found myself thinking of the dancer who was asked to explain her dance. She replied "If I could have done that I would not have danced it."

What I have tried to do here, with a brief outline of the major events of my life, is to set them in context and hope they might help others in the journey along the narrow way of love.

> *Grant us O Lord to know you are with us always, in good times and bad. Amen*

THE NARROW WAY

In my darkest hour,
when sorrow and pain
have sought to overwhelm,
I glimpsed an ancient
settlement
where no harm can be done.

Be not fooled though by
loud proclamations
and expansive vistas.

It is a narrow way
that leads to life
in this ancient settlement
of love.

At the age of 4 I had what I call an "Eternal Moment." I saw nothing, I heard nothing and yet I apprehended the truth of God's love and mercy in a way which defies description and would seem impossible for a small child.

I was adopted at 15 months old and have never known my natural parents. There was a woman who used to visit from time to time and on one occasion she gave me some wooden beads, I realised much later this was a Rosary. I took the beads with me up to the bedroom. It was raining heavily and as I watched the rain I found myself in this "Eternal Moment" in which I somehow knew that Christ was the light that shines in the darkness and the darkness could not overcome him.

As I was held in this moment I knew there were to be dark and difficult times ahead. In the silence of this extraordinary moment it was as though I was asked how I wanted to respond to the difficulties and darkness which were ahead. My reply "keep me from bitterness and resentment" is something I have pondered much as I have sought to travel the narrow way.

It seemed that in some way I knew I could not fulfil this desire myself. I was asking that God would protect me from the wiles of the Evil One, who delights to see people ensnared by bitterness and resentment. I have had to renew this prayer many times as pain and sorrow have sought to overwhelm me over and over again.

Shortly after this moment the Rosary was taken away by my adoptive mother and I never saw it again.

I believe the woman who visited was my natural mother and it was the last time she visited. I cannot verify this as my adoptive family were very reluctant to tell me anything of my natural parents, but piecing together the bits of information I do have this seems very likely to be so.

There are many things in life over which we have no control but we can always choose how we want to respond to events. If we choose to walk the narrow way of love we must put our hand in the wounded hand of Christ, for we cannot walk this way in our own strength. Only by the grace of God can we be the people we were created to be, love made in the image of Love.

"If death has no meaning, then life has no meaning." These words were spoken to me by my father when I was upset about the death of a neighbour and friend. I was 13 at the time and the words made little sense. I stored them away in a pocket of my heart.

My beloved father died two years later and as I wrestled with unbearable grief and confusion I took these words and looked at them again. They still made little sense.

Three years later my mother died. This was a very different sort of grief. Her erratic outbursts of physical abuse along with continuous verbal beatings made her death a relief and welcome parting.

The next blow dealt by death was another three years later when my husband died after we had been married for 15 months. The words spoken by my father still made little sense as I looked at them over and over again.

Thirty years on and my second husband, in the grips of a serious psychotic breakdown, committed suicide in a very brutal manner. Now despite much pain and sadness things were different, the words of my father had begun to take root in my heart and mind. I had learned to stand on my head and look at life differently.

Standing in the healing light of the Resurrection, the green buds of hope grew where once only fear and doubt had flourished. I saw the world sprinkled with the blood of the noon-day passion and all pain and suffering lifted up to God's mercy seat in the wounded hands of Christ.

We do not come to know the reality of hope in the Resurrection of Christ by running away from pain and death but by facing it. It is as we stand at the cross looking on the wounds of Christ that we come to know the God who is love and the reality of life eternal. For Christ said, **"Now this is eternal life: that we may know you, the only true God, and Jesus Christ, whom you have sent."** *John 17.3*

Life and death are indeed forever entwined for it is through the death of Christ that we may enter into the reality of eternal life.

The words of Christ from the cross – *"Father, forgive them, for they know not what they do"* are difficult to accept in the face of abuse and violence.

Being illegitimate in the 1950's was to be an outcast, a second class citizen. There were those who questioned why God allowed children like me to survive when much wanted legitimate children died. I sometimes wondered about this myself.

My adoptive mother had herself lost a son at birth and she clearly had mixed feelings about my survival.

She married again after my father's death and died herself 10 months after her marriage, I was 18. Her new husband was less than honourable. Due to a quirk in the law he inherited all my mother's property and money. With wandering hands and jeering remarks about me being dependent on him, he tried to lure me into his bed.

I packed a bag and left, not knowing where I was going. My sister and her husband were gracious enough to give me shelter until I married.

I was constantly aware of the dark forces of revenge creeping around the rooftops of my mind. Others encouraged me to think this was justified but the words of Christ continued to echo in the dark caverns of my soul. Over and over I have had to renew my prayer "keep me from bitterness and resentment."

When we join in the prayer of Christ – Father forgive ... we tend to find our minds wondering about so many things. How can it be right to forgive this and that. If we continue to repeat this prayer, with a desire for it to be more than words, slowly the prayer moves from the mind to the heart. We find ourselves being drawn closer and closer to Christ and our many questions cease.

We should be in no doubt that hatred, bitterness, resentment and the desire for revenge are not of God. The call to walk along the narrow way of love is not about nice warm fuzzy feelings. It is a call in good times and bad, to walk in the footsteps of Christ, to love our enemies, to pray for those who persecute us and to overcome evil with good.

My child, you are not yet a brave and truly wise
lover of Me.
Why not Lord?
Because when you meet a little difficulty you
fall off from what you have begun,
and you seek consolation too eagerly.
A true lover stands firm in times of trial
and is not deceived by the enemy.
He loves Me as much when things go ill as when
all goes well.
Thomas A Kempis on True Love

AN AUTOBIOGRAPHY

Conceived outside the city walls of law,
an orphan, rescued by love's grace,
raised in the courts of trial and
temptations,
a diligent pupil of life's lessons.

My one desire – to know who I was
and be an upright citizen of the world,
inside the city walls.

Alas, despite my greatest efforts,
I never gained the necessary qualifications:
on the outside I always remained.

Attending the University of Bereavement,
I attained a costly degree of understanding.

Looking backwards, off my guard, my foot
slipped and into the dark and lonely pit
of depression I fell.

A long time waiting in this place,
the gulls of self pity constantly screeching
overhead.

Accepting this might be my dwelling place
for ever, in a moment I knew
I no longer waited alone.

The strangest peace then overcame
all my common sense.
Content to leave or to stay,
I glimpsed a far-off land,
where I was called to go.

Vain and foolish, oft I strayed
as the dark clouds parted.

The sun shone now
as I basked in the joys, and sorrows,
of child bearing,
the rich blessings of God's most
wondrous grace.

As with the seasons, life's rhythms did
ebb and flow. I found myself now closer
to that far-off land I glimpsed so long ago.

Again more wonderful,
and yet terrifying things did I see,
through the binoculars of suffering.

Terrible storms again raged all around me,
with loved ones from far and near
joining in the world's chorus
of disapproval.

Battle-worn and weary from life's bitter attack,
I found solace in the calling
of the Cross.

Life is sweeter now, for I know who I am,
and from whence I came.
On the promise of God's love, through faith,
to my father Abraham I have returned
to be a child of grace.

AT FOUR – AN ETERNAL MOMENT

At four I looked and saw
what was not there.

I was not happy,
I was not sad,
when I found myself in
a place that was not
a place,
in a room that was not
a room.

This place, this room
that was not there,
was not square or round,
high or low.
It was not dark or light.
I saw no windows or doors.
I know not how I entered
or left this place, this room
that was not there.

In this place, this room
that was not there,
a soft and awesome silence
filled the air,
and yet every sort of sound
could be heard.

In this place, this room
that was not there,
I felt both lost and found,
exposed, naked and vulnerable,
but safe, secure and hidden.

I was there but for a moment,
a moment that seemed to be eternal,
a moment it is impossible to leave.

I now knew things I had not known before.
I knew of darkness and light.
I knew of the Light of the World
that could not be overpowered by darkness.

I did not speak of this moment
for I was a child.
I knew no words to explain or
describe this place, this room
that was not there – but I knew
I had been bathed in the mercy
of Christ.

In this place, this room that was
not there, a silent voice spoke of
dark and difficult times ahead.
The silence asked of me,
"How do you want to respond?"
From I know not where,
I heard a voice cry out,
"Keep me from bitterness and resentment."

The moment passed.
I was just a child at play again and yet
it hadn't passed.
Through times of sadness and
joy, faith and doubt, hope and
despair, in sickness and in health,
this moment has remained.

TRUTH

Raising the eyes of my soul
I looked and saw the truth
of eternity.

The truth is Love,
so bright and pure,
keeping my soul forever
near.

To love is truth,
this my soul's desire
as I call out:
"lead me to the rock
that is higher than I."

In eternity was my soul
conceived.
in the truth of Love
it will return.

A FATHER'S DEATH
(Adoptive Father)

Your leaving tore my heart to shreds
and submerged my mind in the
murky mire of dread.

I longed to shout and wail,
to enfold myself in the black
cloak of mourning.
But no – "Silence!" they said,
"Be quiet. Too young are you
for the full dress of mourning."

So cold and desolate,
in grey I stood,
suspended between
the fine white linen of faith and light
and the warm protective black of mourning.

The pain was terrible,
nobody understood.
In denying me the black and comforting
clothes of Friday's mourning,
they also robbed me of the white and
joyful clothes of Sunday morning.

Many days and nights I stood
in these grey half-way clothes
of life and death.
But in waiting I learned the art of
"standing on my head."

Looking at life upside down,
I found that death was not all
she claimed to be,
although she had much to teach
about Love's gift of life.

A WELCOME PARTING
(Adoptive Mother's Death)

I know not what caused you to be
so cold and cruel to me.

Perhaps your own wounds were
too sore to let you give shelter
and comfort to another.

Only Love himself knows your story,
only he can judge.

Your greatest fear –
that I would cause
the shame of Mother Nature to come
knocking at your door.
Your fear became mine
and I grew more and more ashamed
with the passing of each year.

Your instruction I took to heart:
"Do not walk with your head
held high; in the gutter is where you belong."

The wounds you inflicted on my body
are insignificant
when compared to the wounds
your cruel words left
upon my mind.

Even standing on my head
your words and actions were
beyond my ken.

It is sad to say, but for me,
your death was a welcome
parting. But you went having
made no provision for me.
I was left, a young and vulnerable
maiden, at the mercy of your new man.

Left homeless and penniless,
the days and nights that followed
were very dark indeed – but deep
within my soul a tiny flame still
flickered and, through grace,
I staggered on.

As I have journeyed through
the decades since your death,
the healing touch of Christ
has transformed my shame and
self-loathing into love.

I no longer fear to stand up straight
or lift my eyes from the gutter.

I hope and pray that you too have
found Love's healing touch and
that we might meet again, both
forgiven sinners, dancing in the
courts of heaven.
    Amen

STOLEN INHERITANCE
(Stepfather)

You stole my wealth
and my home
then your wandering hands
froze my heart and mind,
allowing you to steal my
innocence and self esteem.

I wanted to shout "Shame on
you, shame on you!"
but my voice was lost in the raging fires
of fear and dread.

Like a refugee I had not time
to gather my possessions
but at the break of day
I had to flee from your shameful
wanton deeds.

Homeless and dejected
I wandered helplessly through life,
drifting from one lost hope to
another.

Lost I might have been forever,
but for knowing there was One
who loved my wandering, lost
and wayward soul.

"Revenge, revenge!" a dark and shadowy voice
often whispered in my mind. Left alone, I
might have responded to this dark and
dangerous desire. But thanks be to God for
His grace, calling me to run from this raging
destructive force.

Sometimes in the night I still
see the shadowy form of revenge
creeping around the rooftops of
my mind.
When challenged, however, with
whisperings of mercy, this cowardly
figure disappears into the swirling
mists of unbelief.

And to you,
the man who stole so much from me,
I know not whether you live or die,
but where'er you be, I pray you too
will know the healing touch of mercy.

THREE MONTHS IN SUMMER LONG AGO

A child still,
but wearing adult clothing,
I tried to be at your side.

The days and nights were hot
and stifling as you shuttled
back and forth between life
and death.

Summoned here and there by
experts in this and that, I tried
to understand their unintelligible
jargon of causes, dire consequences
and narrow margins.

My mind in freefall eventually
landed in the silent marshlands
of numbing despair.

Hospital corridors and waiting
rooms became very good friends
of mine.
With good grace they listened to
my silent screams;
they never offered good advice.

As the final blow of death drew near
these silent screams scurried back
beneath a heavy blanket of ice
as I resumed the frozen face of
common sense.

It was only to meet with the necessities
of life that I left your side
and in that moment
it seemed you chose to go.

Perhaps you couldn't bear the pain
of parting; perhaps you were glad
to go. The answer I will never know.

A widow now, when only yesterday
I had been a bride.

Many years have been and gone
since I tried to be at your side
that summer long ago.
My silent screams have now found
a safe secure resting place for
their release.
And in the silence of my prayer,
at your side I now can be
as you journey on through the
golden starlit courts of eternity.

THE WIDOW

Looking out to sea I asked
"When did this pain begin?"
Others think it was at your dying
but no – it has always been within.

Grief was a welcome relief,
respectable clothing for the
loneliness of sin.

For a while, head held high,
I wore my widow's weeds with pride;
rather quickly though, they wore thin.
Again I was helpless and sorrowful,
facing the loneliness within.

Here and there I ran,
shouting, screaming, weeping, wailing,
building idols large and small.
At any cost I avoided facing again
that dark and lonely pit within.

Guilty of every kind of sin,
day and night I worshipped the
goddess of respectability.
Reigning in mortal splendour,
she took all I had to offer.

Exhausted by her demands,
again I was left facing that large
and empty space within.
The death of a loved one is not
the true reason for my weeping.
Rather, it is the loss of innocence
and truth, exposed at his leaving.

A cruel twist of the law stole it
away. Cold, empty and naked,
now I will face this stark and
painful loneliness within.

CONDEMNATION

They never asked how it was this
situation came to be.
And so the condemnation began.

They knew nothing of the pain of
watching a loved one ravaged by
the paranoid delusions of grandeur.
They knew nothing of one man's
battle with the demons of dependency,
obsession and sin.
And so the condemnation began.

They had only met with the charming
and generous Dr Jekyll.
They had no idea of a wife and children's
terrifying nightly ordeal,
with the bizarre and violent behaviour
of the not-so-charming Mr Hyde.
And so the condemnation began.

They did not want to know the truth
of their idol's struggle – a scapegoat
must be found.
And so the condemnation began.

They continued in their ignorance
spreading falsehood and innuendo,
unaware of the damage they were doing.
And so the condemnation began.

They will never know the part their
wagging tongues played in one man's
violent parting.
It was their very readiness to judge
and condemn
that filled him with such terrifying
dread.
If the truth should out, surely
they would turn on him.
And so the condemnation began.

Factless futile malicious gossip
is the soil in which this condemnation
began.

Father hold not this sin against them.
                                        Amen

A MAN I ONCE KNEW

No words are adequate to describe
the pain of your living death.

The gruesome parasites of paranoia
fed, day and night, on the inner workings
of your mind.
Fear and suspicion stalked your every
thought.

As you searched for relief in the
numbing punches of beer and wine
an alien was born.

Long before you took your body to
its violent death,
the man I once knew had left.

The sense of helplessness in the face
of such dark and desolate despair
was a heavy cross to bear.

Oh, such pain and suffering –
  it stole your mind,
  it stole my reputation,
  it stole the innocence of our children.

And yet, strange it is to say,
it strengthened my belief in the
love of God
to hold and keep for eternity
a man I once knew.

SECOND TIME AROUND

As I wear my widow's weeds
a second time around,
fear and dread no longer
mark my every step.

Pain and loss have taught
me well.

Standing on my head
I see rainbows by night
and starlit skies by day.
The sun shines green with
the light of hope,
the moon is dressed in a
white bridal gown of faith
and every star is sprinkled
with the ruby-red love of
the noon-day passion.

Second time around,
faith and hope lead
on this pilgrimage of life,
and death.

DEATH AND LIFE

Death and life,
always so far away
and yet so near.

One cannot be found
without the other.

Entwined like lovers,
their footprints
stretch back and forth
across the sands of time,
        one forever in eternity.

WHO AM I?

Through storms and gales,
through the gentle breeze of
hazy days,
this question I have asked:
    Who am I?

As a child
and an adult,
sister, daughter, widow, wife
and mother,
this question I have asked:
    Who am I?

On the heights of success,
in the depths of despair,
in the doctor's chair,
on my father's knee,
this question I have asked:
    Who am I?

To the wise and learned,
to the wild and carefree,
to anyone who would listen,
this question I have asked:
    Who am I?

I stopped asking this question,
for no one, it seemed, had the answer
but then
a still small voice spoke, saying
    I AM HE.
Suddenly I knew the answer to
my question.
Through the waters of the Cross
I discovered
    I am not!

STAR OF ABRAHAM

These people who conceived me –
were their hearts entwined in love
    or
were they two lonely ships passing
in the night, dazzled and emboldened
by the festive wine of Christmas cheer?

Did my birth bring sadness and sorrow
    or
bitter rage at such disruption to life?

Did friends and family give comfort
and support
    or
admonish and abandon?

Have their hearts ever searched for me
as mine has searched for them?

For decade upon decade my life has
lain buried beneath this myriad of
unanswered questions.

But now, with thanks and praise
for the life they gave to me,
I must rise from the ashes of this earthly quest,
ascend Jacob's ladder
and find my home among the
stars of Abraham.

In Christ is born the hope
of life eternal.
Amen

PART TWO
The Hippo's Tale
A call to share things seen

That which was from the beginning,
which we have heard, which we have seen
with our eyes, which we have looked at and our
hands have touched – this we proclaim
concerning the Word of life.

1 John 1.1

THE HIPPO'S TALE

As the wind of God's love
lifts me off my feet,
I see the beauty of yesteryear
far, far below,
but also I see the dazzling splendour
of where it is I am to go.

Up and up and up love lifts me,
to gaze upon the delicate grace
of a snowflake's face,
to marvel at the raindrop's gift of music,
to listen to the tale of leaves,
rustling in the wind,
to bathe in the gentle beauty of the risen sun,
to walk along the footpaths of humility,
to dance in the magnificently jewelled
ballroom of obedience,
to rest so peacefully upon heaven's
featherbed of truth,
to sing a song of freedom from the
tallest tree.

Gently does the wind of God's love
put me down again,
with a silent whisper He commands:
"Share what you have seen."

Tentatively I knock at the door of
the hedgehog's abode:
alas his spines are in defensive mode –
he dare not look or listen.
Here comes the peacock.
Perhaps he will listen – too busy
is he with a proud display of his
tail.

The snail will surely want to know –
but no – so paralysed with timidity
he runs into his shell.

The ants I went to next – will they
stop, look and listen?
Far too busy were they to think
of heaven

Lord to whom shall I go?

"Have you met the starling with the broken
wing,
the magpie with one eye,
the toad with a growth on his head
or the spider who has lost a leg?"

Ah Lord, as a hippo with an aching heart,
here I can share the secrets of your love.

WAVES OF MERCY

Speak and act as those who are going to be
judged by the law that gives freedom,
because judgement without mercy will be shown
to anyone who has not been merciful.
Mercy triumphs over judgement.

James 2.12-13

I will have mercy on whom I will have mercy, and I will have compassion on whom I will have compassion.
Exodus 33.19

The extraordinary gift of God's mercy is something far beyond the normal understanding of the human mind.

When the prophet Isaiah was caught up in a vision of the glory of God he said – **'Woe to me! I am a man of unclean lips , and I live among a people of unclean lips, and my eyes have seen the King, the Lord Almighty.** (Isaiah 6.5) Isaiah did not just see the sin of others, he saw his own sin too. Beware of self-righteous Prophets and Preachers who see only the sin of others.

Any true vision or sense of the awesomeness of God's love will always cause us to be more aware of our own sin and that of the fallen world, but not in a negative way. True vision kindles a deep desire for God's image to be restored in ourselves and all humanity.

Our acceptance of God's love and mercy is the foundation necessary if our lives are to become temples of sacred love. To truly live in the light of God's forgiveness and mercy we must die to self, what we think, what we agree with, who we think are worthy of mercy or who should or should not be allowed into the heavenly courts.

The mercy of God is revealed in all its fullness through Christ on the cross. The Cross is the Mercy Seat from which the prayer of Christ – ('**Father, forgive them, for they do not know what they are doing.**' Luke 23.34), rises like incense to the Father.

If we sit at the feet of Christ and listen with open hearts and minds to this prayer we touch something of the glory of God which is beyond all imagining.

Like Job we realise that all too often we speak of things we do not understand, things too wonderful for us to know.

> **You asked, "Who is this who obscures my counsel without knowledge?"**
> **Surely I spoke of things I did not understand, things too wonderful for me to know.**
> *Job 42.3*

MERCY

Mercy, mine to give,
flowing through the river
of love;
the edges shallow,
the centre deep.
Come – wet your feet.

Mercy, mine to give,
to all who tread these waters,
forever yours to keep.
Come – wet your feet.

Mercy, mine to give;
waves may toss and roar
but peace to mine
upon the ocean floor.
Come – wet your feet
in the ocean of God's love.

A PROPHET'S PRAYER

O Lord of my heart,
to thee do I come
when shadows fall
and the light grows dim,
helplessly burdened
with sorrow and sin.
O Lord of my heart,
to thee do I come.

O Lord of my heart,
to thee do I come
with gladness,
humbly accepting forgiveness
and mercy.
In spirit and truth,
to love and to worship,
O Lord of my heart,
to thee do I come.

SILENCE

What of silence?
To some a friend – to some a foe.

The silent frogman
dives deep below the surface of
the mind,
bringing up the subtleties of sin,
buried
in the silt of fear and pride.

To the humble the silent frogman
is a treasured friend,
releasing the soul
to live in harmony
with heaven and earth.

To the proud the silent frogman
is a terrifying enemy,
revealing the deceitfulness of
man's self-will.

The proud – fugitives always on
the run,
trying to escape the sound of silence.
Alas there is no escape,
for silence is not the absence of noise,
but the voice of God.

The humble – freemen of the eternal
city,
their trial is over: 'guilty' was the verdict.
In passing sentence,
the Judge listened to their advocate:
"Father forgive them, for they know
not what they do."

Listen, listen today to the silence of the
Cross.

MADELINE AND THE BEE

Madeline came to tea.
Mother said, "She will be here at three."
In truth she came at noon,
but no one knew
for she had been looking out to sea.

Nobody noticed her arrival
except me.
She was very, very small
and accompanied by a bee!

She climbed the steps;
almost at the top she tripped and fell
on one knee.
There she stayed awhile,
watching lords and ladies
drinking tea.
Without a sound she rose,
still accompanied by the bee!

A sweet but powerful perfume
seemed to emanate from her nose.
Then she turned and looked
straight at me.
She took me by the hand, whispering,
"Come and see."
My heart fluttered in hesitation –
I was afraid of the bee!

Gently she led me across the crowded
terrace
to sit beneath the shade of the apple
tree.
Her perfume soothed my anxious thoughts
and I no longer feared the bee!

*(Deborah – Judge and Leader of Israel
the name 'Deborah' means 'bee'.)*

TOPSY TURVY LOVE
(The Chair of Peter)

Lord,
How topsy turvy your love is,
for it is in the darkest places of my heart
that I find the brightest light of your love.

But oh, how easily is the heart of man
deceived.
To weep over my own poor soul was
humility, I thought;
but whilst my ego was off guard,
I discovered this was pride – not
humility at all!

What a waste of time to weep over my sin
when I could instead
proclaim the greatness of thy mercy.

"Produce fruit in keeping with repentance!"
the Baptist cried – acknowledgment of
sin, acceptance of forgiveness;
this is not the fruit, but the seeds from
which the fruit will grow.

The fruit of repentance: a change of
direction – no concern with me,
not even my sin!
but a life lived in thought, word and deed
only to tell of the glory, the splendour and
the majesty of Christ my Lord.
      Amen

RIGHTEOUS MEN

What of the righteous men
who oppose that human babe
from heaven?

Each face unique,
beautiful as a snowflake,
with a frozen laugh
and eyes that never
smile.

What of the righteous men
who oppose that human babe
from heaven?

At Sunday's dawn
the living waters of the skies
will fall
and the snow will be no more;
then righteous men
with saints and sinners
on bended knees will fall
in worship
of that human babe from heaven
who is
Christ the Lord.
                Amen

BATTLE

O Lord
take this heart of mine
to restore and make like thine,
forever giving of love divine.

O Lord
the enemy strikes by day and
night.
Clothe me in your battledress
of love and mercy,
your word
my sword with which to fight.

O Lord
take this heart of mine
that therein the light of victory
might shine
for all the world to see.

A PENTECOST PRAYER

O come pure and mighty dove,
the wood of salvation in thy
beak,
enter my mortal flesh
and create for thyself
a temple of sacred love.

Furnish my soul
with cries of delight,
open wide the windows
of humility
that I might gaze upon
the truth of thy love for me.
                    Amen

SHEPHERD OF OUR HEARTS

Dear Shepherd of our hearts,
leaving all to find the weak and lost;
in the mercy of thy flesh
thou didst carry us home
on the victory of thy cross.

Dear Shepherd of our hearts,
by thy sheep
thy voice is known;
through the mercy of thy flesh
all may now enter heaven.

Dear Shepherd of our hearts,
at thy ascending,
thy Holy Dove's empowering;
by the mercy of thy flesh,
on earth as in heaven,
man shall reflect the beauty
of thy face.
    Amen

WATERS OF LIFE

Mercy, the sound of silently-flowing
waters of life,
brought forth
by the piercing of His side.

The sword
reveals heaven's glory,
bathed in the mercy of His blood.

Only the lips of faith could proclaim,
in the darkness of death,
"Surely, this man was the
Son of God."
       Amen

SCARLET CLOAK

Enfolded in the scarlet cloak of
divine mercy,
the fallen world waits
for that time beyond
time
when she will again shine
with the resplendent glory
of the One and Only.

A NAME

Mercy, Mercy,
Mercy is thy name,
source of life,
fountain of all goodness.

Mercy, Mercy,
Mercy is thy name,
redeemer of souls,
ocean of perfect love.

Mercy, Mercy,
Mercy is thy name,
victor of darkness,
light of the world.

Mercy, Mercy,
Mercy is thy name,
glory of the heavens,
silence of eternity.

Mercy, Mercy,
Mercy is thy name,
holy, eternal,
beyond all knowing.

Mercy, Mercy,
Mercy is thy name.

THE VOICE

From the mountains
to the valleys,
down sunny glades
and darkened paths,
the voice of Christ,
    my Lord,
is calling:
Father forgive – for they know not
                what they do.

Across the roar of mighty oceans,
from the highlands
to the nations all,
the voice of Christ,
    my Lord,
is calling:
Father forgive – for they know not
                what they do.

In the joy of dawn's awakening,
until the close of evening's call,
the voice of Christ,
    my Lord,
is calling:
Father forgive – for they know not
                what they do.

GOLDEN LIGHT

Far beyond the understanding
of the human mind
the golden light of mercy shines.

The boundaries of time,
penetrated by beams of mercy's
golden light, dissolve, releasing
captives from the limitations of
worldly knowledge.

Ready now to be carried across
the rivers and streams of earthly
wisdom
to the mountain home of Love.

New beginnings and new horizons
unfold in this ancient, eternal
temple of sacred love.

The language of idle speculation
and curiosity is no longer spoken
by those who reside in this holy land.

The mysterious music of silence
engages the mind with
hitherto unsung sonnets of praise and
adoration.

Earthly plains now shrouded
from view,
the golden light of mercy,
moment by moment,
reveals the eternal splendour
of Love's grace.

Far beyond the understanding
of the human mind,
the golden light of mercy
shines.

THREE PAST NOON

At three past noon
the tide turns
and gentle waves of mercy
lap the shores of time.

With ardent passion
the blood-red ocean of
Love Eternal
swallows the moving sands
of deceit.

The sound of glory is carried
on the wind,
singing to a fractious world
a love song of life everlasting.

Glory Alleluia – Amen

MURDER IN THE PARLOUR OF THE MIND

**But now a righteousness from God, apart from law,
has been made known, to which the Law and the Prophets
testify. This righteousness from God comes through
faith in Jesus Christ to all who believe. There is no difference,
for all have sinned and fall short of the glory of God,
and are justified freely by his grace through
the redemption that came by Christ Jesus.**

Romans 3.21-24

He has performed mighty deeds with his arm; he has scattered those who are proud in their inmost thoughts.
Luke 1.51

The characters of fear, envy, sloth, compromise and pride portrayed in the following words may seem rather amusing but they are deadly serious. They are all masters of disguise and play their part in all the wars and conflicts of the world, large and small, as they do in all personal conflicts and cruelties.

'*All have sinned and fall short of the glory of God*' – it is all too easy to pay lip service to these words and as we do so, pride, the deadliest of sins, murders the truth of God's perfect love for us and all people.

Evil's cunning deceit and humanity's sin in all its awfulness, is revealed on Calvary as darkness covered the land. In the darkness the light of Christ continued to shine in his trust of the Father and his prayer for forgiveness. His light continues to shine in the midst of darkness and nothing can overcome God's perfect love, revealed in Christ, for this fallen world and all his people. **The light shines in the darkness, and the darkness has not overcome it.**
John 1.5

In many ways the mystery of God's love leaves us perplexed. Mystery is about something hidden, not fully understood.

The disciples struggled to understand why Christ did not call upon the legions of angels (Matt.26.53) or use his miraculous powers to avoid his arrest and murder. We too struggle in many ways as we wonder why God allows trouble and strife. To the world it is a strange thing that the fullness of God's love is revealed through our sin, it is a mystery, a mystery that is revealed not through study and debate, but by love alone.

If we are to be made perfect in love we have to die to self and turn to Christ.

Pride seeks the riches of self-righteousness, humility stands in the poverty of truth, clothed in the grace of forgiveness and mercy knowing it is not the righteous Christ came to call.

> **Jesus said, "It is not the healthy who need a doctor, but the sick. But go and learn what this means: I desire mercy, not sacrifice. For I have not come to call the righteous, but sinners.**
> *Matthew 9.13*

MURDER

In the Parlour of the Mind
lies the corpse of Truth,
strangled by the illusions of
false humility.

Whose hands are stained
with the victim's blood?

Fear and Envy must surely
be prime suspects,
but what of Compromise and Sloth?

Each suspects the other.

The clues are few;
tracks have been well covered
but wait – upon the body,
disguised as honesty
the Holy Detective of Discernment
has found the fingerprints
of Pride.

Justice now will be done:
Pride's kingdom will fall
by the sword of Love's word.

THE HOLY DETECTIVE OF DISCERNMENT

The Holy Detective of Discernment
always walks in the sovereign truth of Love,
robed in a scarlet cloak of mercy,
banishing the dark clouds of condemnation
with songs of silent adoration.

With a loud voice,
the promised restoration of Eden's glory
is proclaimed,
and Pride's mighty and majestic illusions are
slain;
and the whisperings of the wind
carry the delicate fragrance of humility
to the farthest corners of the land.

A DOUBLE AGENT

Fear – once an agent of wisdom –
defected to serve Pride.

Under the cover of darkness
she weakens all defences,
opening the doors and windows
of the soul
to all agents of sin.

Rich and poor,
strong and weak alike
she targets.
With cunning deceit
she knocks them off their feet.

Leaving her victims sick and frail
with the perfume of charm
she covers her trail.

LADY FEAR COMES TO STAY

Lady Fear,
an expensive guest to entertain.

Humility, wisdom and discernment
she finds an appetising starter.

A main course of truth and
sincerity she devours
without a backward glance.

Joy and peace make a perfect
dessert.

All washed down with a glass
of deceit
chilled to perfection.

Leaving you to pay the bill,
into the night she vanishes.

LOOKING GLASS

Tripping through the ages,
looking glass to the fore,
the just and noble cause of
Cain is upheld.

Soldiers clothed in green
demand now –
    a Saracen's head,
    a bourgeois poet's voice,
    the life of a gentle man,
    meek and mild.

At the turn of every tide
the purifying blood of Abel
cries incessantly from the
ground – as again and
again
the spoils of false hope
ravage the beauty
of the human mind.

MADAM ENVY

With a charming mask of flattery
she disguises her venomous
hissings of spite and rage.

With eloquent words,
advocating the noble causes
of 'equality and justice,'
she blinds her conquests
and leads them into the
stinking mire of hypocrisy.

Hypocrisy – the meanest sin:
all fair without and foul within.
Gilbert of Sempringham

COMPROMISE

Compromise is a hearty fellow,
always serving the needs of his
fellow men with good cheer.
He fears the loneliness of truth.

With an awkward smile
he wears the fashions of the age.
Bending this way and that,
he accommodates scoffers and
self-righteous hypocrites alike.

Compromise is a hearty fellow,
manipulated by fear and doubt,
flattered by the deceitful words
of envy and spite.
Anchorless, he is tossed hither
and thither on stormy seas
and then washed ashore
on the lukewarm beaches of
mediocrity.

SLOTH

Sloth,
a brilliant performer,
always at his best in days of war,
portraying so convincingly
the virtues of wisdom,
keeping a silent watch
over the ravages of sin.

Sloth,
a private person;
with the rewards of self-preservation
he barricades himself in.

THE WATCHDOG OF PRIDE

With incessant zeal the Watchdog of Pride
guards the rebellious heart.
With dogged determination he
refuses entry to the meek and gentle
Lamb of Love.

On the bones of 'the law' he gnaws
day and night,
salivating with relish at the downfall
of another.
Worshipping the gods of self-righteousness,
he sacrifices the bread of mercy
for the spoils of self-satisfaction and hypocrisy.

A blind guide,
he leads blind men into the treacherous
pit of despair.

THE MUSIC OF REVENGE AND PUNISHMENT

Throughout the long days and nights
of Pride's reign,
the dark and dangerous music
of revenge and punishment
beats out across the rooftops
of the mind,
drowning out the light
of Love's silent song.

Beware dear friends,
take care,
for this music
fragments the mind
and sedates the soul.

Beware dear friends,
beware.

TURN DEAR FRIENDS

Across the world
in the homes of the
rich and powerful,
the poor and weak,
the fiendish friends of
Pride are regularly
entertained
in the Parlour of the Mind.

In servile arrogance
they hold court;
debating and analysing,
sitting as judge and jury,
they hand out life sentences
of servitude and drudgery.

Turn dear friends,
turn again and appeal
to the highest authority
in the land – the Lord of Love,
the Lord Most High.

From his Mercy Seat
he will overturn this sentence
with the free pardon of Calvary.

FRIDAY'S KISS
(Matthew 12)

Lips cut and bruised,
his body cruelly scourged,
Love bent down and kissed
the world
with words so pure and true:
>"Father, forgive them,
>for they know not what they do."

In some this kiss arouses a thirst for life,
awakening memories of different
horizons,
a knowing of new beginnings beyond
the boundaries of time.

In others this kiss arouses shouts
of righteous indignation,
threatening the illusory power of
man-made barons,
entrenched in the pretentious
echelons of time.

Many others know nothing of this
kiss;
they stagger through their days
searching for love,
dazed and numbed by the endless
beatings of despair.

Love does not quarrel or cry out
in the streets,
a bruised reed he will not break,
a smouldering wick he will not
snuff out.

Until the days of time cease
he will continue to kiss the world
with the wine of his blood,
leading justice to victory,
and in his name will the nations
put their hope.

THE CROSS

I know a place
where heaven meets earth,
where pain and death
meet
with the joy of life.

This place – the Cross.

Where a king meets
with sinners,
where thieves and prostitutes,
righteous men
and holy virgins
share one cup.

This place – the Cross.

An invitation to a banquet
has today been sent to
you – will you come?

RSVP – THE CROSS

THE PROMISE TREE

The sun is almost down.
The night-time shadows of revenge
and punishment
dance upon the delicate mosaic
of the human mind.

At the dead of night
how many will be cracked
by the constant pounding of the beat?
So, so many souls with whom to weep.

Too late to stop the music of the night;
all are lost in the silent slumber of defeat.
Where, oh where, on such a night
is shelter to be found?

Beneath the rainbow-coloured leaves
of the Promise Tree.

Silently, angels of mercy carry the
wounded and the dead
to the Physician of Heaven.
From the Cross
he heals the wounds of sin
by his mercy
and raises the dead
in the waters of eternal life.

TAKE MY FACE
A Prayer for Healing

Praise the Lord, O my soul;

all my inmost being, praise his holy name.

Praise the Lord O my soul,

and forget not all his benefits—

who forgives all your sins

and heals all your diseases,

who redeems your life from the pit

and crowns you with love and compassion,

who satisfies your desires with good things

so that your youth is renewed

like the eagle's.

Psalm 103.1-5

Heal me O Lord, and I shall be healed; save me and I shall be saved, for you are the one I praise.
Jeremiah 17.14

Jeremiah does not praise God because he has been healed, he seeks healing and salvation from the God whom he praises regardless.

The restoration and healing we all need is that of the right relationship to God. Praise and adoration are at the centre of this right relationship not only because of what God has done but because of who he is.

God is love and we are made in his image. His love is unfailing and unconditional. When we allow ourselves to be held in God's unfailing, unconditional love, letting go of all the demands of our ego-self, finding that place of true poverty and surrender, we begin to find our sadness and pain being transformed into the wine of joy and gladness. This is not the false joy of human effort brought about by denying our pain and sadness and putting on a brave face. It is the joy of knowing that nothing can separate us from the love of God in Christ, the joy of knowing the One true God, which is eternal life – **Now this is eternal life, to know the only true God and Jesus Christ whom he has sent.**
(John 17.3)

When we live in the truth of God's unfailing love our praise and adoration is no longer conditional, we praise him in sunshine and rain, in gladness and pain.

Whatever is happening, however dark it may be, however confusing and painful life may be we live enfolded in the peace of God which passes all understanding.

The kingdom of God is not of this world, it is not out there in dreamy starlit skies: it is within us. It is a place of freedom where we are no longer captive to the demands of self or the values of the fallen world. It is a place of joy and hope, the hope of life everlasting.

"The kingdom of God does not come with your careful observation, nor will people say, 'Here it is,' or 'There it is,' because the kingdom of God is within you."
Luke 17.21

TAKE MY FACE

Take my face,
        dear Lord,
and make it thine,
to shine with the beauty
and the wisdom
of your cross.

Take my face,
        dear Lord,
and make it thine.
Take the sadness
and the pain
and turn them into wine.

Take my face,
        dear Lord,
and make it thine.
In this world
let it be an icon
of your everlasting love.

        Amen

THE ROAD

Oh, the foolishness of men,
hearts forever yearning,
but struggling, on we go.

A wayside inn to rest,
to drink and eat,
but no – ever searching,
on we go.

Could it be we missed
the road?
My head says No,
my heart says Yes,
but in pride on we go.

Did we turn to left or right?
The road is straight and narrow
the old man said.
Back on the road now,
a little late,
but on we go.

In the distance we see the
destination we desire,
sometimes running,
sometimes crawling,
but in hope, on we go.

CAPTIVITY

How beautiful
in the early morning dew
is the prison of the spider's web;
such are the outward charms
of captivity's lair.

Once caught,
to fight and struggle will bring
certain death
as the finely woven web
of deceit
tightens its grip.

The only hope now of escape
is for the web to be broken.

Oh joy! Oh joy!
Love's sword has now brought
freedom.

JOURNEY INTO SILENCE

Ascending
with heavenly joy
through the starlit skies
of faith and hope
to wait upon the morning light
of surrender.

Stepping out of the grave-clothes
of independence
to be showered by the
gently-cascading waters
of silence.

Enraptured,
my heart and mind
danced in the nakedness of truth
to the symphony of holiness
beating out
across the hills and meadows
of eternity.

SURRENDER

Pride was the leprosy of my soul,
eating away, disfiguring,
a sight unbelievably grotesque.
The rotting flesh of my soul
filled the air with the stench
of arrogance.

At the midnight hour
my voice grew louder and louder,
demanding to know – why, why, why?
My ego, like Caiaphas, sent
    Almighty God
to be tried by Pontius Pilate.

O my soul, what hope for you?
So sick,
death only a moment away.
My only hope:
to find the Holy Physician –
he alone could heal me.

In sack cloth and ashes,
mounting my faithful steed
(dear Faith),
I rode through the night
until I found his abode –
  the stable of humility
  hidden beneath the night-time sky –
with only the star of belief to guide me.

At dawn,
tired and weary I arrived,
hesitant as I knocked;
he opened wide his arms to
greet me.
Leading me inside,
he ordered rest.
With his Spirit
he kissed the disfigured and
rotting flesh of my soul.
The fragrance of his wounds,
like frankincense,
overcame the stench of my
arrogance.

Slowly healing comes
as I learn to be still and rest.
Some days now
I can laugh at
the foolishness of my pride,
always asking why.
Then with a shudder
I remember how close I came
to death.

Never does he speak of days
gone by,
but bathes my wounds with the
balm of now.

It is with awe that I lie on the
shores of time,
my soul longing for the silence
of complete surrender,
when, in his arms, I know he will
carry me into the silent ocean of
eternity.

MINUET IN G

Held in the awesome mystery
of love,
nothing moves.
Days and nights are lost
in the secret touches
of this embrace.

Moments of glad grace
  dance a minuet
in the caverns of the mind,
  applauded
by the ancestors of the heart.

Grant O God
my mind not to wander
down the winding paths
of rebellion.
Lead it ever on
the narrow road of surrender.
                    Amen

PROMISE FULFILLED

A promise fulfilled to a maiden
rare
for a world,
languishing
in the murky waters
of despair.

A promise fulfilled to a man
golden and fair,
scourged and betrayed
for the sin of the world
laid bare.

A promise fulfilled to those who
follow there,
in surrender,
the Holy Dance of Love
to share.

GOODBYE TO DESPAIR

The sun is green,
teeming with life ....

Who pays for life with blood
blue and true?

A prophet,
a man,
a king?
No – no payment is made
for life:
it is a gift to be received.

Payment is made for death
and oh, how costly it is.

The sun is green,
teeming with life.............

A chill wind pours forth –
there is talk of rain.
Tomorrow is Friday again.

Walking on glass,
hands full of stones to throw –
cats and dogs
fear hell lies below.

Praise to the gods of Vanity Fair
and to the men and maidens
who worship there.

The sun is green,
teeming with life ....

Goodbye dear friends,
goodbye one and all.
I must take my leave
and journey on
through the land where
day is night
and darkness light.

The sun is green,
teeming with life ....

SEARCHING

How weary is my soul
from its searching for love –
fear and doubt ever in pursuit.

Pausing at the stile of surrender,
I see self-will and understanding
jeering, with lecherous smiles,
waiting to ravage my mind.

O sweet Jesus,
I will pause no longer,
but ask you to tie my hands of self-will
with cords of love
and to close my eyes of understanding
with the kiss of your Spirit.

Unable now to defend myself,
on the authority of
your hand alone will I rely.

O sweet Jesus,
lead me home,
there to rest and receive
the blessings of
your Mass.

GATES OF ETERNITY

The golden gates of eternity,
ablaze with the flames of love,
are approached
by the narrow path of humility;
there to wait
in silent trust
till the battle of noon is won
and the passions of self-will
are laid to rest
in the tomb of poverty.

POVERTY

Gracious Lord,
in whose name we walk
and have our being,
with such a tender heart
you call us to rest
in poverty's tomb.

To leave the opulent mansion
of independence
with its ceaseless demands
and such an outward show
of grandeur.

Trust is the lining of poverty's
tomb –
heart and mind,
  the will of the flesh
surrendered to the Spirit's embrace.

At home now
  in rags or riches,
the journey to Calvary
we are ready to begin.

Dear poverty,
be ever my companion
on this long and lonely road.
  Amen

A CELEBRATION OF POVERTY

Nothing now do I own –
not even my sin –
for on Calvary
Christ took it as his own.

In return
he gave to me
the precious gift of life
eternal.

Through his song of poverty
the power of sin was broken
and joy now abounds on earth.

The air is filled with the fragrance
and tenderness
of his eternal embrace.

SONG OF CREATION

Lord,
as today I stood cold and naked,
you enfolded me
in the blanket of creation.

My heart strangely warmed
as, like salt
cleansing my wounds,
your love penetrated my mind,
melting fear's icy grip.
             Amen

THE ADVENT OF SPRING

How still creation stands
on this rainy day,
an air of expectancy in
her silent song.

The winter trees are clothed
today from on high
with a shimmering cloak:
the waters of baptism
bedecked
with jewelled raindrops of faith.

This cloak
hides not their nakedness
but restores the beauty of innocence
as they await the birth of Spring.

These trees,
some tall and slender,
others short and round,
all stand majestic in their faith.
Even as night approaches
they know very soon
the Lord of heaven and earth
will fulfil his promise of new life,
dressing them
in the lush green garments of hope.

UPON A CLOUD

Today upon a cloud
I saw the voice of God
moving on ahead.

I saw Him whisper to the
heavens above and the
earth below:
Come follow me.

In His voice I saw the body
of the soul,
yesterday, today and tomorrow.

As He spoke I saw the rib from
which I came and how as He
whispered with His hands I
returned again.

Passing by on the other side
I saw a messenger of the Lord
calling through the clouds to
man:
Renounce, renounce and come on high.

Today upon a cloud
I saw the voice of God
moving on ahead.

FREEDOM

On the wing of the mighty dove,
into the night I flee,
moving so, so quietly,
disturbing not
the sleeping shadows of the mind,
but joyously homeward bound.

How long a prisoner there,
chained by fear and doubt?
But in the darkness
as they lay sleeping,
I crept out.

As daylight dawns
a mighty search begins –
to no avail,
for disguised, as one,
above the clouds we sail.

BLUEBELLS IN WINTER

Songs of a Soul
In Winter

"Men cry out under a load of oppression;
they plead for relief from
from the arm of the powerful.
But no one says, 'Where is God my Maker,
who gives songs in the night,
who teaches more to us
than to the beasts of the earth
and makes us wiser than the birds of the air?'"

Job 35.9

There is a time for everything, and a season for every activity under heaven. *Ecclesiastes 3.1*

As my life descended into ever deeper difficulties I was surprised to find myself singing the prayers in this section. I have no musical training, do not know a 'b' from a 'c' and know nothing about musical composition. I just found myself singing them.

We pay much attention in our world to the mind and body but what of our soul ? What indeed is the soul ?
I believe it to be who we really are . In the Gospel Christ says –
Do not be afraid of those who kill the body but cannot kill the soul. *Matthew 10.28*

We tend to live very much at the surface level of our minds and understanding but there is much, much more to life than our minds can understand. There is within us a deep place of silence, the silence of trust where the love that is God is apprehended in a way far beyond words. From this place of silence we see the fallen world through the wounds of love, we see the sin of the world defeated and life restored by the blood of love. Held in the arms of God's mercy we gaze upon the mystery of life eternal and find ourselves adorned with jewels of faith, a priceless gift of grace.

We see our lives as pure gift as God breathes upon us to bless us with his peace which passes all understanding, causing us to cry out with a deep desire – *Live your life in me Lord, take possession of my soul Lord, live your life in me.*

The silence of trust calls unto the Lord with a passion for all humanity to be set free from the snares of the enemy and to know the truth of God's unfailing love for all.

This is love: not that we loved God , but that he loved us and sent his Son as an atoning sacrifice for our sins. Dear friends since God so loved us, we also ought to love one another. No one has ever seen God, but if we love one another, God lives in us and his love is made complete in us.

1 John 4.10

CLEANSE MY HEART

Storms of anger, hatred and self-righteous
indignation erupted in my mind.
Blizzards of doubt and unbelief pounded
at the door of my heart, so it was with great
relief that I found my soul singing:

Cleanse my heart O God,
sanctify my soul,
anoint my lips
with the fragrance of
your name.
Jesus Christ is Lord.
Glory be to God.

WEEPING

As I walked through these long dark
 nights of winter,
listening to the song of silence,
I watched the worries and cares
of this life
 ensnaring a sleeping world.

Looking out
upon the valley of the shadow
of death,
my soul was overwhelmed
by what I saw:

I saw the Lord weeping,
weeping for his people,
weeping for his people.
I saw the Lord,
I saw the Lord,
I saw the Lord.

BREATH OF GOD

As the thunderous clouds of condemnation
rumbled around the rooftops of my mind,
I found myself
looking through the ages,
upon the ravages of death.
Bodies, bodies, bodies
littering the landscapes of
history
and the ages yet to come.
Touching the void of death's
desolation,
my aching weary bones
cried out:

Breath of God most holy,
breath of God most holy,
breath of God most holy,
grant us life.

LAMB OF GOD

The icy cold winds of fear
clouded the reasoning of
my mind – but then,
looking to the left of my
understanding,
on the threshold of life,
I saw the multi-coloured
music of the Word,
kissing the universe,
sharing the silent
sounds of
Love's passion.

In joyous rapture
my heart and mind sang:

O Lord
Lamb of God,
Lamb of God.
Life restored
by the blood of love,
by the blood of love.

Hand in hand,
man with God.

BY YOUR WOUNDS

Seeking shelter from these winter storms,
I found a hiding place in the wounds of Christ.
As I rested there,
a still small voice fluttered in my soul,
calling me to look beyond the boundaries of time.
As I looked through the wounds of
Love, I saw a universe transformed.

Here, stars sang in unison,
whilst birds of prey cut off their feet of clay
and jackdaws thieved no more.

Behind the curtains of death
lilies grew in the most unexpected places
and, glistening in the midday sun,
raindrops of eternity
streamed down awestruck faces.

The paralysing spell of fear was broken.
With unbridled passion,
living stones cried out:

By your wounds,
by your wounds,
heal us, heal us
O Christ.

LIVE YOUR LIFE IN ME LORD

With every passing day
the grip of winter tightened.
My strength was ebbing away.
I had spent myself in the
good works of vanity and pride.

Without the strength or desire
to attend any longer to the
demands of self-will,
they passed by,
like ants marching on parade
as my soul prayed:

Live your life in me Lord,
live your life in me.
Take possession of my soul Lord,
live your life in me.

IN YOU O CHRIST IS MY LIFE

Awakened from a restless and agitated
sleep,
I was carried on the gentle wings of Love
across the frontiers of time,
to gaze upon the beauty and wonder
of life,
enfolded in the music of the Word,
a symphony of love,
written before the world began.

Lost in this moment of eternal
mystery,
new horizons came into view.
Love lifted me so high,
I touched the stars and watched
raindrops formed in clouds of
Love unknown.

Forever touched with wonder,
a song of remembrance stirred
in my heart:

In you O Christ is my life,
is my life.
Amen Amen Amen Amen

IN THE ARMS OF THE LORD

It was late winter.
Heavy snow was falling
and the lights were beginning
to flicker
when I felt a gentle
but persistent
prompting in my spirit:

"What do you ask of the Lord?"

In an instant, words escaped from
my mouth, like captives released
from jail:
"To dwell in the house of the Lord
all the days of my life."

I waited with bated breath.
I feared presumption,
but yet more words now escaped
and a peace, defying description,
enfolded my heart and mind as
my lips sang:

I will rest in the arms of the Lord,
I will rest in the arms of the Lord.
Alleluia! Alleluia! Alleluia!

LIFE ETERNAL

At the peak of winter's icy blast,
standing on the mysteries of faith,
looking heavenward:
the world's primordial cry of despair
echoed in the unlit caverns of my soul.

With outstretched arms
the light of love
reached into the darkness
of this cry,
bringing forth echoes of praise,
rising like incense from
ages past.

In these caverns,
now ablaze with the
light of the Incarnate Word,
a song of hope can be heard:

In Christ, in Christ, in Christ is born
the hope of life eternal.
In Christ, in Christ, in Christ is born
the hope of life eternal.

Amen, Amen, Amen, Amen,
the hope of life eternal.

SILENTLY I STAND

On a cold frosty morning
out of the blue it came – the most minute,
yet ever expanding emerald space,
festooned with the
treasures of cosmic hope
and eternal silences.

In the distance
ancient sites of divine glory shine
in the silvery light of grace.

Deeper and deeper
the light of the Holy Eternal Word
penetrates this ever-expanding
emerald space,
causing my heart to
sigh with songs of silence:

Silently I stand,
silently I stand,
silently I stand before the Lord,
before the Lord, before the Lord most high.

My silence calls,
my silence calls,
unto the Lord my silence calls.

JEWELS OF FAITH

During this long hard winter I received
an anonymous gift of precious jewels.

I asked of Love:
"From where did these precious
jewels come?"

It was the wind that answered:
"They are your inheritance
of grace."

Surprised and delighted,
I offered these jewels
as a sacrifice of praise
on the altar of love:

Jewels of faith I bring
to thee my king,
jewels of faith,
that they might adorn,
that they might adorn
thy crown of glory,
thy crown of glory,
Christ my King.

THE HOURS

A Voyage of Love

**And now these three remain: faith, hope
and love.
But the greatest of these is love.**

1 Corinthians 13.13

There is no fear in love. But perfect love drives out fear, because fear has to do with punishment. The one who fears is not made perfect in love. *1 John 4.18*

A regular rhythm of prayer is a daily voyage of love in which we rejoice in the truth that every day is a new beginning remembering that love keeps no record of wrongs.

The world, constantly on the run, is ensnared by the fear of death. Prayer leads us to Calvary to look upon love's defeat of death and listen over and over to the Victory song of love – Father, forgive them for they know not what they do.

As evening comes and the daylight of reason and understanding begin to fade causing us to cry out, Where is God? Why has he forsaken us?, prayer leads us into the truth, that he is with us always, in joy and sorrow, in life and in death.

At the close of day, with praise and thanksgiving, in the bounty of God redeemed sinners stand and pray that all would know the joy of sins forgiven.

A song of silence fills the air, foolish fears and delinquent doubts are banished as we are bathed over and over in waves of mercy which flood our hearts and minds with the hope of life everlasting as we rest in the arms of Christ.

> **Many are asking, "Who can show us any good?"**
> **Let the light of your face shine upon us, O Lord.**
> **You have filled my heart with greater joy than when their grain and new wine abound.**
> **I will lie down and sleep in peace, for you alone, O Lord, make me dwell in safety.**
> *Psalm 4.6-8*

VOYAGE OF LOVE

"Come away, come away with me,"
my Lord did cry.
"Let us sail to the Land of Love."

With great delight I rushed to and fro,
my luggage ready, eager to set sail,
when I heard my Lord's voice calling,
"NO – take no luggage on this voyage."

Confused and disappointed,
I left behind the clothes in which I
looked so good,
my books of wisdom
and all my pearls of great price.

Again I heard my Lord's voice calling,
"Come, take my hand."
His voice I heard
but his face I could not see,
for by this time darkness had fallen.
Unsure of my ground,
tears of fear pricked my eyes,
when, without warning,
he caught me in his arms.

Silently he carried me to the water's
edge:
there, hidden among the bulrushes
our royal yacht was waiting.
As we left the harbour
I heard the owl's hooting –
"Is it wise to sail at night
without provision for the journey?"
but as we journeyed and I pondered
on the beauty of the night-time sky,
the owl's hooting we left behind.

For hours and hours
my Lord was silent
as we watched and waited
for the wind to come.

As the night grew darker,
the doubts and fears of my mind
became ever more exposed.
Forgotten memories,
like enemy soldiers ready to shoot,
were constantly on the horizon.
But, in reaching out my hand
and calling to my Lord,
these enemies began to disappear.

Becalmed in the middle of life's
mighty ocean,
more than once I almost capsized the boat
with my restless agitation.

And where, oh where now is
my Lord,
as all my senses fail me?
His voice I do not hear,
His face I do not see,
His hand I do not feel,
His wine I do not taste:
and yet
the strangest thing I found –
the invisible hand of faith upheld me
and calmed my
troubled mind.

My yearning for dawn slowly waned
as I lay contentedly in the night's
embrace,
feeding on the delectable mysteries
of faith.

How long it was I lay there I do
not know
but without warning,
again I heard the voice of my Lord calling,
"Awake, awake,
for soon daylight will be dawning."
The sky now changing,
the curtains of darkness are parting
and on the distant horizon lies the
Island of Hope.

As we approached this island,
the depths of the ocean's pollution
became much clearer.
All manner of dirt and waste
I now could see beneath the
ocean's surface.

But a moment passed, it seemed,
until we docked at Love's harbour.
And oh what joy as we disembarked,
for here, my Lord shared with me
the fullness of his love
and gave to me his cross.

Together now, hand in hand,
we can walk in this land,
obedient to the Father's will.

In this land time stands still,
the crops never fail,
a song of silence fills the air,
the trees are laden with good
things to eat,
as we share the nuptials of love,
as is our Father's pleasure.

MATINS

The Lord God formed the man
from the dust of the ground
and breathed into his nostrils the breath of life,
and the man became a living being.

Genesis 2:7

Breath of God most holy, grant us life.

Amen

DAWN

Dawn approaches;
the fears and doubts
of night diminish.

On the horizon,
glimmering like drops
of dew,
beyond the shores of
selfish pride,
lie the jewels of faith
and trust.

Priceless jewels,
not to be stored away,
but to wear,
through which the sunlight
shines,
revealing the Father's pleasure.

THE HOPE OF HEAVEN

The hope of heaven lies within
the heart;
through the eyes of a child it
is glimpsed.

With the stillness of dawn
the beauty of hope comes
into view.

Anchored in faith,
even as dark clouds gather,
the beauty of hope will
never fade.

NEW BEGINNINGS

New every morning
bright as the sun
God recreates us
each and every one

Sing Alleluia
Sing Alleluia
Sing Alleluia

Praise to the Father
Praise to the Son
Praise to the Spirit
three in one

SEXT

**"Look, the Lamb of God,
who takes away the sin of the world!"**
John 1:29

O Lord, Lamb of God,
life restored by the blood of love.
Hand in hand, man with God.

HOPE

A child,
dying in the night.
A young man weeping
at love's parting.
A mother's heart
filled with fear.
An old man's dreams
fading fast.

Running from east to west,
wise men,
kings and princes,
vagabonds,
ladies of the chamber
and sailors –
searching, searching
for hope, so long since lost.

Where, oh where is hope to be
found?
Hope, my child,
is not to be found in living,
but in dying.
Hope, so long since lost,
is found
in Love's offering
upon the Cross.

THE GRAVE

Even the grave must yield
to the victory of love.

Man, put to sleep by the
ravages of sin,
in the twinkling of an eye,
as the trumpet sounds,
will rise to new life,
awakened by the Spirit's
kiss.

O death, where is your victory?

O death, where is your sting?

WINGS

On rainbow-coloured wings of
light
the world's desperate cries of
night
are carried to the majestic
heights of Calvary – there to
be held
in the wounds of Love's
eternal sacrifice,
until new day dawns,
the buds of hope flower
and the lamb lies down with the lion.

VICTORY SONG

In the palm of his hand
the Father's love
holds and protects
his lambs.

Father, forgive them,
for they know not what they do.

From the palm of his hand
the Son's love
pours forth the victory
song.

Father, forgive them,
for they know not what they do.

By the palm of his hand
the Spirit's love
is imparted to one and
all.

Father, forgive them,
for they know not what they do.

BEYOND

The mountains of the mind
are forever shrouded
with mist,
rising from the valley of
the shadow of death.

To the east,
beyond Friday's icy peak,
beams of pearlescent light
penetrate the hardened
ground of fear and doubt.

A voice cries out:
"My Lord and My God."
       Amen

VESPERS

In him was life,
and that life was the light of men.
The light shines in the darkness,
but the darkness has
not overcome it.

John 1:5

In you O Christ is my life.

Amen

DARKNESS

Daylight is fading,
the moon creeping into view,
doubts and fears
tapping
at the window pane.

Do not rush to close the
curtains,
to put on artificial lights,
but sit and wait........................
....
.....................be still,
and your eyes will grow
accustomed – not to darkness,
but to the sun's reflected
light.

New sounds to hear,
new things to see,
there you will find
Love's ever-guiding light.

DUET

As the day draws to the end
and night-time comes,
I, your Lord, am near.

As the air is filled
with songs and praise,
in the silence of your prayer,
I, your Lord, am near.

As you strive and strain
and then at last to rest,
I, your Lord, am near.

As you journey onwards,
fast or slow,
I, your Lord, am near.

As you rise to take your
place
in my Father's house,
I, your Lord, am near.

WATER INTO WINE

Love speaks to love
made in his own image,
an echo of himself.

At his wedding feast,
with a silent caress,
Love changed water
into wine,
calling forth new life
from death.

Love speaks to love
as day speaks to light
and the moon echoes
through the night.

HOSPITALITY OF INTERCESSION

There are strangers in my heart
Lord,
needing shelter from the relentless
storms of this moonless night.

With the wood of your cross
Lord,
stoke the fire of love in the hearth
of my soul,
that I might offer to these strangers
a royal welcome,
melting the icy grip of fear and pride.
                Amen

COMPLINE

I will lie down and sleep in peace,
for you alone, O Lord,
make me dwell in safety.
Psalm 4:8

Father, may my sleep be in the arms of Jesus.
May my dreams be of heaven
and may my waking be in the joy and hope
of eternal life.
Amen

THE BOUNTY OF GOD

In the bounty of God
redeemed sinners stand.

Robed with the light of the stars,
crowned with raindrops of mercy.

In the bounty of God
redeemed sinners stand.

*   *   *

In the bounty of God
redeemed sinners stand.

Songs of gladness and joy
fill their days
as they approach the golden
gates of Calvary,
entering into death and
everlasting life.

In the bounty of God
redeemed sinners stand.

BATTLE CRY

Let the arms of God's love
hold you in the darkness.

Let the life of God's Son
lead you into light.

Let the mercy of Jesus Christ
be shared with all.

FIRE

Hearts of love,
yielding with desire,
consumed by flames
of holy fire,
entering into glory
and everlasting light.

Welcomed in,
ever there to stay.
Flames of holy love,
burning with delight,
to wound,
to cherish,
to soar above the night.

MILLENNIUM MOMENT

A thousand nights
passing through the gaze of love.

The grace of morning dew
bathing mortal feet
with wine.

Upon the mountain peak
heaven embraces earth
with the kiss
of eternity – as tomorrow
shines
with ageless beauty
across the skies of risen
glory.

PRAISE BE TO GOD

Praise be to God
      for the morning,
unfolding and spreading the
      light of new day.

Praise be to God
      for the silence of heaven,
enfolding the wounded earth
      in its gaze.

Praise be to God
      for his Christ,
his beauty and splendour
      casting out the gloom of
night's candour.

Praise be to God
      for his being.

Praise be to God.
      Alleluia
      Amen

WORSHIP

A true heart,
freely given to worship thee,
shall not,
by time nor place,
by man nor beast,
ever be bound.

Endless love it gathers in
to give in service
in the dark and distant
wilderness.

From morn till night,
even as the cock doth crow,
a true heart
is free
to worship thee.

O AWESOME MYSTERY

A Holy Dance of Love

Praise the Lord.
Sing to the Lord a new song,
his praise in the assembly of the saints.
Let Israel rejoice in their Maker;
let the people of Zion be glad in their King.
Let them praise his name with dancing,
and make music to him with
tambourine and harp.
For the Lord takes delight in his people;
he crowns the humble with salvation.
Let the saints rejoice in this honour
and sing for joy on their beds.
Psalm 149.1-5

Simply let your 'Yes' be 'Yes' and your 'No', 'No'; anything beyond this comes from the evil one.
Matt.5.37

Behind the awesome mystery of Christmas, God born in human form, is the 'yes' of a young girl . It was a 'yes' which led her through dangerous and difficult places. Joseph initially was not convinced that this was of God but following a dream he, as the disciples would do later, left home and all his own plans behind in order to dance with God. Wise Men followed a star and Shepherds responded to the message of the Angel, left their flocks and hurried off to Bethlehem to see this extraordinary thing that had happened.

The events of that first Christmas reveal a group of people who were prepared to 'lean not on their own understanding' (Proverbs 3.5) but to trust God and respond to the promptings of the Holy Spirit. In so doing they joined in God's Holy Dance of Love – a dance which had and continues to have profound affects upon the world.

The call is to dance with God, not for him, learning to move in time with his plans, remembering that a thousand years is but a day in the sight of God (*Psalm 90.4*)

The voice of God is a still small voice which is easily drowned out by the voice of our own thoughts and ideas and those of the world.

Hidden within each of us lies the deep desire to dance with God for that is what we were created to do. In countless, obvious and not so obvious ways, we still listen to the whisperings of the serpent, so often disguised as wisdom, who hides among the weeds of fear and doubt in the garden of our souls.

Saying 'yes' to God does not guarantee a trouble free life. On the contrary, Mary risked being stoned to death, had to give birth in a dark, damp cave and stood at the Cross watching her son being crucified. Eleven of the twelve disciples were martyred. Our 'yes' has consequences far beyond this world, it is a 'yes' to die to self that we might live in the awesome mystery of God's unfailing love now and throughout all eternity.

Praise be to you Father, Praise be to you Son
and Praise be to you Holy Spirit. Enfold us and
all creation in the mystery of your grace that we
might join your Holy Dance of Love.
    Amen

O AWESOME MYSTERY

From north to south
the wind blows,
changing the hidden landscapes
of the mind.

O awesome mystery.

Tides of time pushed back
by the omnipotence
of eternity.

O awesome mystery.

The majestic beauty
of a mother,
revealing the hope of
heaven's glory.

O awesome mystery,
    awesome mystery.

TO DANCE

Listen first to the rhythm of
the music.

Let every step be in time
and every pause
a gift from heaven.

Take to the floor
and dance the night away
in the magnificently jewelled
ballroom
of obedience.

MARY – THE MOTHER OF GOD

In purity and obedience she bore him,
watchful in his growing years.
In purity and obedience she followed,
grief and joy to suffer there.

In trust and adoration she came before
him,
Almighty God for all to see.
In trust and adoration,
his shame, his death, his glory
there to see.

In glory and honour she was united
with him
as one in love, his work to share.
In glory and honour,
with joy and peace in life eternally.

WOMAN OF STONE

Not at an altar she stood,
but at the foot of the cross.
Not with her lips did she preach God's word,
but in her life she gave him birth.

"Blessed is the womb that bore you."
"Blessed is the one who hears the
Word of God and keeps it."

Blessed is she among women,
shrouded in mystery, clothed in humility,
ready to serve the one to whom she gave birth.

No stranger was she to the sovereign hand of God,
ready to say Yes to him to whom the
world and its captives say No.

A wife, a mother, a prophet of God,
the handmaid of the Lord.
All generations shall call you blessed,
Mary, the Mother of God.

Now safely entombed in tablets of stone,
her Yes to the Lord and No to the world
is outdated it seems; and the Lord whom she bore,
God revealed in human form,
is no longer adored.

JOSEPH

Joseph,
a man content to be led.

Protector of life,
giving of love,
silent in mystery.
A man of stature
content to be led.

Dancing by day,
watching by night,
believing and trusting,
guided by light.

Joseph,
a man content to be led.

NO ROOM AT THE INN

Upon that Holy Night
for whom was there
'no room at the inn'?

The homeless, the poor,
the rejected and lonely?
             No.
It was those who had heard
the word of God
and obeyed it,
for whom there was
no room at the inn.

Blessed are they,
blessed are they for all
eternity.

A WINTER'S NIGHT

From heaven he came
upon a winter's night,
to walk amongst his people
here on earth below.

Bringing the Father's love
to weak and strong alike,
that each of us might know
the mercy of his grace.

Into the darkened world
came the Father's wondrous
light,
his own precious Son,
our Lord Jesus Christ.

THE INCARNATION

A withered hand, an unclean spirit,
man paralysed by sin – the air is
putrid with the fumes of man's
decaying flesh.

Hope is fading fast.

A dark and starry night,
a different smell now is in the air –
frankincense and myrrh.

Trumpets sound, shepherds stop
and stare –
"Good News for man and beast,"
they say.

As the world lay helpless in its
despair, clothed as man,
to earth God came to stay.

Lame men walk, blind men
again can see – the air is sweeter
now than words can tell.

A tiny helpless child has brought
to earth
heaven's gift of eternal life.

HOLY NIGHT

In the silent watch of the night,
the awesome sound of mystery
is glimpsed
on the threshold of dawn.

The moon and stars bow down
their heads,
shepherds rejoice,
wise men follow a star
and angel voices call to the
nations all:
> Come see, come see!
> The light of heaven to earth has
> come.

NEW JERUSALEM

On distant shores a loud
silence,
crystal clear and radiant,
descending through the
heavenly realms.

On earth raindrops of
morning light appear.

In the east a guiding light
is seen.

Wise men seek and find
the Alpha and the Omega,
the Holy City,
the New Jerusalem.

The heavenly tent,
pitched on earth amidst
a crown of stars.

MORNING STAR

Lightened by the light
of lights,
the world awakens
to the music of the
bright morning star.

A symphony of mystery,
piercing the earthly strata,
whispers in the wind:
Glory to God in the highest,
     and on earth peace, good
          will toward men.

GOLD, FRANKINCENSE AND MYRRH

Gold
To worship and adore
is the trumpet's call.

To lay at love's feet
the things I count most precious:
loved ones, young and old,
cherished days of yesteryear,
hopes and plans for the morrow,
castles and cottages,
chattels and carriages,
aspirations and talents,
reputation and status,
all that is gold to me.

That is the wise man's response
to the trumpet call.

Frankincense
To worship and adore
is the trumpet's call.

To place into the hands of love
my gift of frankincense:
the truth of my sin,
my heart divided by the tyrannical
forces of fear and doubt;
to acknowledge love's victory
over death.

That is the wise man's response
to the trumpet call.

Myrrh
To worship and adore
is the trumpet's call.

To look into love's face,
bringing my bitter-sweet life
of myrrh,
given in the darkness of Gethsemane,
with the hope of restoration in the
fullness of Eden's glory.

That is the wise man's response
to the trumpet call.

To worship and adore,
bringing gifts of gold, frankincense
and myrrh,
wise men came.

To worship and adore,
bringing gifts of gold, frankincense
and myrrh,
I come.

BETHLEHEM PRAYER

Dear Lord,
be born this day in the
stable of my heart.

May I follow the star
like the wise men of
yesteryear,
to come and worship
you.

I lay my life at your feet
to be given in service
for all those for whom
there is
no room at the inn.
          Amen

BOATS

In the depths of night,
when the tiger sleeps
and scarlet raindrops
light the way,
I see those boats
left on the shore,
two thousand years
ago, and more.

They speak, these boats
of faith and hope,
of men leaving all
to follow a Shepherd
King from a distant land.

They wait these boats,
for you and me
and for all who will
come to be.

In the darkness they whisper
"we are the starting place,
the beginning of your journey
home,
to the dwelling place of love
and the joys of life eternal."

YES DEAR LORD

Yes dear Lord,
let your life be born in us.

May we stand at the foot of
your cross,
bearing the pain of love,
rejected and slain.

Yes dear Lord,
let your life be born in us.

May we walk in the victory
of your cross,
sharing the joy of love,
risen and glorified.

Yes dear Lord,
let your life be born in us.

May we offer to the world
the victory of your cross,
sharing the life of love
now and forever.

Yes dear Lord,
let your life be born in us.

A MEETING

As I lay resting
in the arms of love,
I found myself
entering that long-forgotten
place,
where I am not.

There I met with Mary,
the Mother of God.
Long, long ago
we had met before
in that long-forgotten
place,
where I am not.

We did not speak
but embraced in a moment
of mutual recognition
in that long-forgotten
place,
where I am not.

SYMPHONY

Hidden deep within every heart
lies a symphony of loving
obedience,
waiting to be played.

Each moment
a note of unique sound
from the orchestra of mankind.

THE CHRIST CHILD

Beyond the frontiers of the mind
lies a foreign land
where day is night
and night is day.............

      and

the purple scented mystery of
Christmas is ever beckoning.

All is still in this land;
only silence speaks
the name of life – born this day
in the stable of eternity.

This land has no temple
and is lit only by the glory of God,
wrapped in swaddling clothes,
lying in a manger............

      and

the voices of:
      a murderer named Moses,
      an adulterous king named David,
      a spotless maiden named Mary,
      a lying apostle named Peter,
      a woman of ill repute named Rahab,
      a repentant thief
      and all the company of heaven
      cry as one:
      "HOLY, HOLY HOLY
      is the lamb that was slain."

A SONG OF ADORATION

Listening to my heart,
I hear a song
dancing on the distant hills
of eternity.

This song listens through
the night
and pirouettes across the plain
by day.

Like the choir of lilies
it does not toil or spin
but dances in the gentle breeze
of life.

Across the skies it echoes;
from age to age
it waltzes through the walls
of time,
as martyrs, red and white,
sing and dance their silent
song of adoration,
accompanied by the harpsichords
of heaven.

A VISIT

In awesome silence
Love's ravishing
transported me
through the mists of desire
to worship
in a great Cathedral in the sky.

Up and beyond the moon,
the stars and sun,
to the dwelling place of love.
For no more than a second
may mortal man enter here.

Nothing less than love,
pure and white,
ever will enter into this
     Holy Dance
of Father, Son and Spirit.

No words, no symbols,
nothing on earth or in heaven
will ever express this awesome sight.

Not by thought, by word or deed,
but by love alone
may mortal man glimpse
the beauty, the splendour and the majesty
of the Godhead
     upon his throne.

For this reason I kneel before the Father, from whom the whole family in heaven and on earth derives its name. I pray that out of his glorious riches he may strengthen you with power, through his Spirit in your innermost being, so that Christ may dwell in your hearts through faith. And I pray that you, being rooted and established in love, may have power together with all the saints, to grasp how wide and long and high and deep is the love of Christ, and to know this love that surpasses all knowledge – that you may be filled to the measure of all the fullness of God.

Now to him who is able to do immeasurably more than all we ask or imagine, according to his power that is at work within us, to him be glory in the church and in Christ Jesus throughout all generations, for ever and ever.
Amen

Ephesians 3 14–21

www.ingramcontent.com/pod-product-compliance
Lightning Source LLC
LaVergne TN
LVHW091255080426
835510LV00007B/266